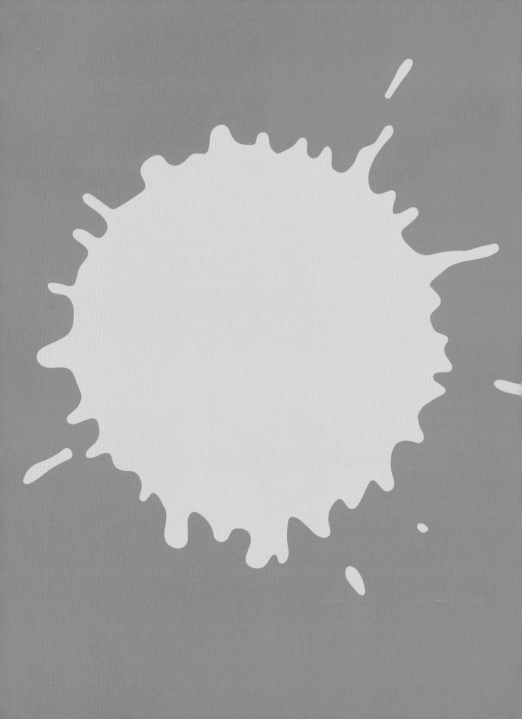

DID YOU KNOW?
Meerkat

DID YOU KNOW?

Meerkat

young reed

Contents

What is a Meerkat?

- The Meerkat is not a 'cat' but a species of **mongoose**.

- Its scientific name is *Suricata suricatta* and an alternative common name for the Meerkat is the '**suricate**'.

- Meerkats have a long, thin body and grow to about **thirty centimetres** long, plus a twenty-centimetre tail.

- They live for up to **fifteen years** in captivity, but usually a bit less than that in the wild.

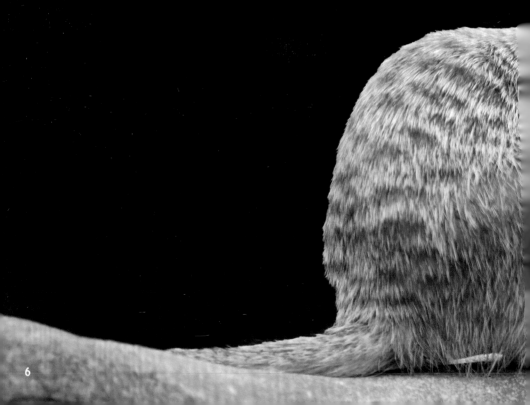

● The wild population of Meerkats is thought to number **half a million** animals.

● Meerkats **don't need to drink** — they get all the water they require from their food.

Where do Meerkats live?

- Today, captive Meerkats are a familiar sight in **zoos and animal parks** all around the world, where they have become a favourite attraction for millions of people.

- In the wild, however, Meerkats live only in certain drier areas of southern Africa, mainly in **South Africa, Botswana** and **Namibia.**

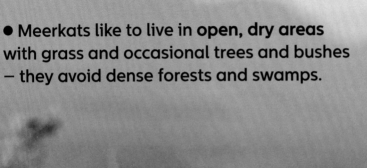

● Meerkats like to live in **open, dry areas** with grass and occasional trees and bushes — they avoid dense forests and swamps.

● They like places with **sandy soil** in which they can dig burrows and search for food.

Family life – mob rule

- Meerkats are very social – they live in a group of up to forty animals that is known as a **gang** or a **mob**.

- Usually one of the older females is the **leader** of the mob and has most of the babies.

- Meerkats are **diurnal** – they are active by day and sleep at night.

● Young Meerkats are born underground in a **den**.

● They measure **seven centimetres** at birth and usually start to explore the world outside the burrow after about **three weeks**.

● The **whole of the mob** works together to find food and shelter and protect the young, which are looked after by their brothers, sisters and cousins, as well as by their parents.

What's for dinner?

● Meerkats are **omnivores**, meaning they eat both plants and animals — including insects, spiders and lizards — with the help of their sharp teeth and claws.

● They are fearless hunters and will take on potentially dangerous prey such as **scorpions and snakes,** using their skill and quick reactions to avoid being bitten or stung.

● If they do get stung they have some **immunity** to the venom.

Territory matters

- A Meerkat mob has a **big territory**, which can be anywhere from four to twelve square kilometres depending on how much food is available.

- Within that territory there is a large **network of burrows**, which are used for various purposes such as sleeping and looking after babies.

- There can be tens of different **sleeping burrows** within a territory — each with many chambers and sometimes hundreds of entrances, all **built over many generations** of Meerkats.

● At the other end of the scale are small **boltholes** used to escape from predators. In its territory a Meerkat is rarely less than forty metres from safety.

On the lookout

- Meerkats are famous for performing **sentinel duties** to look out for and detect potential predators.

● Standing upright, sometimes in a low bush for a better view, they take it in turns to **watch for danger** while the rest of the mob feeds.

- **Warning calls** from the Meerkat sentinel indicate to the group that danger is approaching.

- **Different types of calls** are given depending on whether the threat is from the air — such as an eagle — or on the ground — for example, a monitor lizard.

First published in 2025 by
New Holland Publishers
Sydney

newhollandpublishers.com

Level 1, 178 Fox Valley Road, Wahroonga, NSW 2076, Australia

A record of this book is held at the National Library of Australia.

ISBN 978 1 92107 389 2

OTHER TITLES IN THE 'DID YOU KNOW?' SERIES:

Kangaroos
ISBN 978 1 92107 386 1

Koala
ISBN 978 1 92107 387 8

Lizards
ISBN 978 1 92107 388 5

Penguins
ISBN 978 1 92107 390 8

Red Panda
ISBN 978 1 92107 391 5

For details of these books and hundreds of other Natural History titles see newhollandpublishers.com

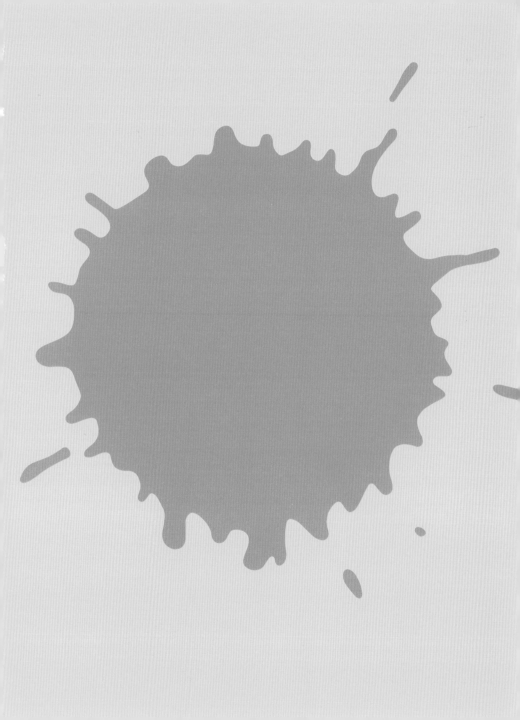